PROJECT GEMINI

A TRUE BOOK

by

**Diane M. and
Paul P. Sipiera**

D1497348

Children's Press®
A Division of Grolier Publishing

New York London Hong Kong Sydney
Danbury, Connecticut

Gemini
space suits

Subject Consultant
Peter Goodwin
Science Department Chairman
Kent School, Kent, CT

Reading Consultant
Linda Cornwell
Learning Resource Consultant
Indiana Department
of Education

Authors' Dedication:
To David L. Williams—
a very good friend who will
always be remembered

Library of Congress Cataloging-in-Publication Data

Sipiera, Diane M.
    Project Gemini / by Diane M. Sipiera and Paul P. Sipiera.
    p. cm. — (A true book)
    Includes bibliographical references and index.
    Summary: Highlights the accomplishments of the twelve missions of
the Gemini Program, including the first manned space flight and the first
extravehicular activity or walk in space.
    ISBN 0-516-20441-6 (lib. bdg.)   0-516-26274-2 (pbk.)
    1. Project Gemini (U.S.)—Juvenile literature. [1. Project Gemini (U.S.)]
I. Sipiera, Paul P. II. Title. III. Series.
TL789.8.U6G68   1997
629.45'4'0973—dc21
                                                          96-50002
                                                             CIP
                                                              AC

Contents

The Space Race — 5

The Gemini Spacecraft — 9

The First Flights — 16

Orbiting Twins — 24

Problems in Orbit — 31

The Final Missions — 36

Project Gemini — 42

To Find Out More — 44

Important Words — 46

Index — 47

Meet the Authors — 48

The United States and the Soviet Union both wanted to be the first country to put a person on the Moon.

The Space Race

At the end of the 1950s, the United States and the Soviet Union were competing with each other in space exploration. This competition was later known as the "space race." The Soviet Union was the first country to place a satellite into orbit around the earth (in 1957) and to put a person in orbit (in 1961). By the early 1960s, the United States was behind the Soviet Union in space exploration.

In 1961, President John F. Kennedy set a goal for the United States. He challenged the National Aeronautics and Space Administration (NASA) to place a person on the Moon before the end of the 1960s. The Soviets also hoped to get to the Moon first.

In a 1961 speech, President John F. Kennedy held up two fingers to show that the United States was running second in the "space race."

NASA's plan to reach the Moon consisted of three separate projects—Project Mercury, Project Gemini, and Project Apollo. The goal of Project Mercury (1958–63) was to prove that humans

After the success of the Project Mercury astronauts (seated), NASA chose astronauts to participate in Project Gemini (standing).

could survive and work in space. Project Apollo (1967–72) would carry astronauts to the Moon. Project Gemini (1964–66) served as a bridge between Mercury and Apollo.

The Gemini Spacecraft

The spacecraft that had been used for Project Mercury had to be changed and improved for Project Gemini. The Gemini spacecraft was larger because it needed to hold two astronauts. It had two parts: the capsule, which carried the astronauts, and a rear area,

The Gemini capsule (bottom) was much larger than the Mercury capsule (top).

which held the reentry rockets. The spacecraft weighed almost 8,000 pounds (3,630 kilograms) and was 18 feet 4 inches (5.6 meters) long. Its base was 10 feet (3 m) across.

The *Titan II* rocket that would launch it into space was 109 feet (33 m) tall.

Gemini had several new features. Fuel cells replaced the batteries that were used in the Mercury capsules to provide more power. The spacecraft also had better computers to help it make more complicated changes in its orbit. Gemini could move forward, backward, and sideways. It could catch up with a target rocket or another space capsule. Gemini truly was a spacecraft piloted by the astronauts.

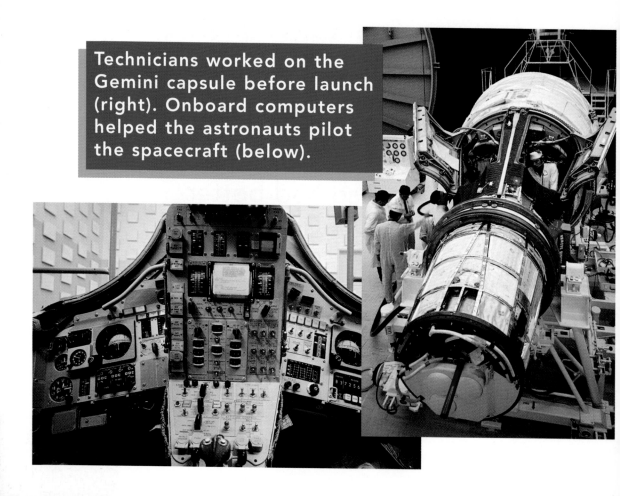

Technicians worked on the Gemini capsule before launch (right). Onboard computers helped the astronauts pilot the spacecraft (below).

Another big difference between the Gemini and Mercury capsules was Gemini's two hatches. These doors could be opened from the inside by the astronauts. This was necessary because the astronauts had to work outside the spacecraft. In Project Mercury, the astronaut was sealed into the capsule, and the hatch could be opened only from the outside after the astronaut returned to Earth.

Project Gemini

Gemini IV
White and McDivitt

Gemini V
Cooper and Conrad

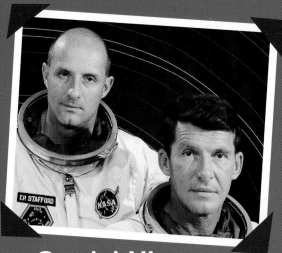

Gemini VI
Stafford and Schirra

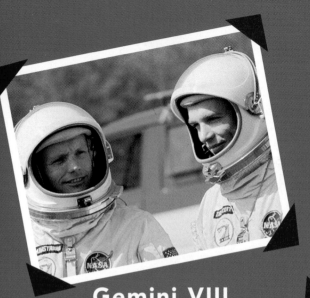

Gemini VIII
Armstrong and Scott

Gemini IX
Cernan and Stafford

Mission	Astronauts	Launch Date
Gemini 3*	Grissom and Young	March 23, 1965
Gemini IV	McDivitt and White	June 3, 1965
Gemini V	Cooper and Conrad	August 21, 1965
Gemini VII	Borman and Lovell	December 4, 1965
Gemini VI	Schirra and Stafford	December 15, 1965
Gemini VIII	Armstrong and Scott	March 16, 1966
Gemini IX	Stafford and Cernan	June 3, 1966
Gemini X	Young and Collins	July 18, 1966
Gemini XI	Conrad and Gordon	September 12, 1966
Gemini XII	Lovell and Aldrin	November 11, 1966

* The use of Roman numerals for missions began with Gemini IV.

The First Flights

The first flights of the Gemini spacecraft had no people on board. They were unmanned missions to test the capsule and rocket. Everything went as planned, and NASA was ready to try the first manned flight.

On March 23, 1965, astronauts Virgil (Gus) I. Grissom

The powerful Titan rocket launched *Gemini 3* into space.

and John W. Young were launched in *Gemini 3* into orbit around the earth. They tested the way the spacecraft

17

Almost five hours after their launch, Grissom and Young splashed down in the ocean, and the capsule was retrieved.

moved by changing its orbit several times. Their three-orbit mission lasted almost five hours and proved that the spacecraft worked well.

The next launch, *Gemini IV*, took place on June 3, 1965, carrying astronauts James A. McDivitt and Edward H. White II on a four-day mission. Their goal was to catch up with a

McDivitt and White make their way to the launch pad.

section of the Titan rocket that had launched them into space. This was a difficult task, and they had to give up because they were using too much fuel. But they did learn valuable lessons in piloting the spacecraft.

The most exciting part of the *Gemini IV* mission was White's spacewalk. White opened the hatch and drifted around the spacecraft (attached by a line) for twenty-one minutes. He

A strong line attached White safely to the capsule during his historic spacewalk. His special space suit cost $26,000.

used a device that looked like a spacegun to help him move around more easily. White was having so much fun that he had to be ordered back into the capsule!

21

Gemini V was in good shape after reentry (left). Astronauts Cooper and Conrad are checked one last time before their flight (below).

MCDONNELL

NASA planned longer missions to see how well the astronauts and equipment would perform. The mission of L. Gordon Cooper Jr. and

Charles (Pete) Conrad Jr. in *Gemini V* lasted almost eight days and made 120 orbits. *Gemini V* was the first flight to use the new fuel-cell power system. The astronauts performed seventeen science experiments and made five changes in orbit before their capsule safely splashed down in the Atlantic Ocean. Their mission proved that astronauts could survive long enough in space to get to the Moon and back.

Orbiting Twins

One of the most important goals of Project Gemini was to prove that two spacecraft could find one another and join together, or dock, in space. *Gemini VI*'s mission was to find and to dock with an orbiting Agena target rocket. But on October 25, 1965, the rocket blew up, leaving astronauts Walter (Wally) M. Schirra Jr. and Thomas P. Stafford without a mission. The next mission, *Gemini VII*, was to be

Schirra (above) and Lovell (left) were originally on separate Gemini missions. But because of an accident with the target rocket, the missions were combined.

On the Gemini missions, the food was freeze-dried. The astronauts just had to add water.

launched in early December and was planned to last fourteen days. NASA decided to combine the two missions. *Gemini VII* would be the target for *Gemini VI*.

Astronauts Frank Borman and James A. Lovell Jr. were

launched in *Gemini VII* on December 4, 1965. They performed twenty science experiments and tested new, lightweight space suits. But the high point of the mission was their meeting with *Gemini VI.*

On the day of *Gemini VI*'s launch, Schirra and Stafford had a frightful experience. Just as their rocket began to fire, it shut down. There was danger of an explosion. The astronauts remained calm, and the mission was saved. Three days later, on December 15, 1965, *Gemini VI* was launched successfully.

It took Schirra and Stafford three orbits and seven changes in orbit to catch up with Borman and Lovell in *Gemini VII.* Shouts of joy were heard as the two spacecraft approached each other. At one point, they were less than 1 foot (.3 m) apart. They remained close to each other for five hours. *Gemini VI* returned to Earth first, and

The *Gemini VI* astronauts spotted the *Gemini VII* capsule (above). The capsules stayed close to each other for five hours (left).

Gemini VII followed three days later. The success of this twin mission was an important step to the Moon.

29

Astronomy

Astronomy is the study of objects in space—their size, color, the way they move, and what they are made of. All of the Gemini astronauts had to study astronomy, because they would need to identify certain stars while in space. They also would need to use the stars for navigation—just like sailors guiding their ships at sea.

Problems in Orbit

Minor problems were common on most missions, but people began to think that space might not be that dangerous. The next two Gemini missions proved, however, that dangers in space were very real.

The mission plan for *Gemini VIII* was to dock with an Agena target rocket. Astronauts Neil

A. Armstrong and David R. Scott were launched on March 16, 1966. After they docked with the rocket, trouble began. The combined spacecraft began to spin out of control! After separating from the rocket, the Gemini capsule began to spin even worse, making one rotation every second.

During their seventh orbit, Armstrong and Scott steadied the spacecraft and made an emergency reentry. The astronauts' training paid off, and

The launch of *Gemini VIII* (left) and the astronauts' safe return (right)

they splashed down safely in the Pacific Ocean. Although both astronauts survived the dangers of space, they suffered from seasickness while waiting for the ship to pick them up!

33

The next mission continued to practice docking with the Agena rocket. *Gemini IX* was launched on June 3, 1966 with Thomas P. Stafford and Eugene A. Cernan on board. They were able to locate the target rocket, but then problems began. A protective covering on the Agena rocket made docking impossible.

There was still much to be done. Cernan worked outside the spacecraft. During his spacewalk, heat built up inside

Gemini IX was able to locate the Agena rocket (above), but docking was impossible. *Gemini IX* splashed down in the ocean (left).

his space suit. His helmet became fogged, and he could not see out. He had to be pulled back into the space-craft. Despite all the problems, Cernan spent more than two hours outside the capsule.

The Final Missions

The final missions of Project Gemini provided more experience for both the astronauts and NASA. These last three missions continued to practice docking, spacewalks, and changing to higher orbit.

John W. Young and Michael Collins were the crew of *Gemini X*. They were launched

Gemini X successfully docked with the Agena rocket (left). Collins practiced with his camera during training (right).

on July 18, 1966, and remained in orbit for almost three days. The highlight of their mission was Collins's spacewalk to the Agena rocket. It was a difficult task, and Collins lost his camera. Other

37

than that, the mission was a complete success.

The *Gemini XI* mission also lasted about three days. The crew was Charles Conrad Jr. and Richard F. Gordon Jr. Much of their work was practice for the future moon missions.

Gordon gets ready for his flight.

Gemini XI sent out a line to the Agena rocket before docking.

The highlight of their mission was reaching a distance of 850 miles (1,368 km) from Earth, farther than anyone had gone before. They also made the first totally computer-controlled reentry.

39

Lovell and Aldrin's flight was the last Gemini mission.

Gemini XII was the final mission. James A. Lovell Jr. and Edwin (Buzz) E. Aldrin Jr. were launched on November 11, 1966. They spent almost four days in space. The lessons learned from the earlier missions were put to good use on their flight.

40

Walking in Space

Spacewalks were an exciting part of the Gemini missions. At first, the astronauts who worked outside the spacecraft had trouble moving around. But by *Gemini XII*, improvements were made. Handrails were attached to the outside of the capsule for astronauts to hold. New ways of preparing for spacewalks also were developed, such as training underwater. Buzz Aldrin made his spacewalks look easy because of his many hours of practice.

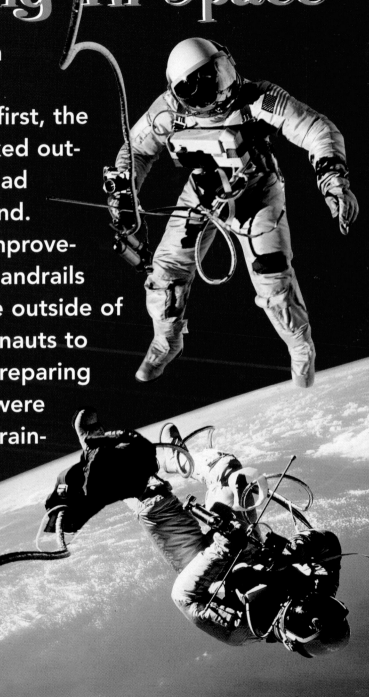

Project Gemini

After *Gemini XII*, NASA had gained enough experience to launch a moon mission. Astronauts had spent almost two thousand hours in space. NASA had developed space-craft able to work in space for up to two weeks.

Although there were some problems left to be solved,

The knowledge learned from Project Gemini, such as docking with other spacecraft while in orbit, prepared the astronauts for trips to the Moon.

Project Apollo could begin. The United States was now winning the space race. Astronauts would soon be on their way to the Moon.

43

To Find Out More

Here are more places to learn about space exploration:

 Books

Abernathy, Susan. **Space Machines.** Western Publishing, 1991.

Kerrod, Robin. **Spacecraft.** Random House, 1989.

Kerrod, Robin. **The Children's Space Atlas.** Millbrook, 1992.

Simon, Seymour. **Space Words: A Dictionary.** HarperCollins, 1991.

Sipiera, Diane M. and Paul P. **Project Mercury.** Children's Press, 1997.

 Organizations

The Planetary Society
65 North Catalina Avenue
Pasadena, CA 91106
(818) 793-5100
http:/planetary.org/tps/

NASA Teacher Resource Center
Mail Stop 8-1
NASA Lewis Research Center
21000 Brookpark Road
Cleveland, OH 44135
(216) 433-4000

National Space Society
922 Pennsylvania Avenue SE
Washington, DC 20003
(202) 543-1900

44

National Air and Space Museum
Smithsonian Institution
601 Independence Ave. SW
Washington, DC 20560
(202) 357-1300

Online Sites

The Children's Museum of Indianapolis
http://childrensmuseum.org/sq1.htm

Visit the SpaceQuest Planetarium to see what it has to offer, including a view of this month's night sky. It can connect you to other astronomy Web sites, too.

History of Space Exploration
http://bang.lanl.gov/solarsys/history.htm

This site has a helpful timeline of space exploration and tells the history of the spacecraft and astronauts.

Kid's Space
http://liftoff.msfc.nasa.gov/kids/welcome.html

Space exploration is really fun at this Web site. Find out how much you would weigh on the Moon, play games, solve puzzles, take quizzes, read stories, and look at the gallery of pictures drawn by kids. Find out how you can post a drawing online, too!

NASA Home Page
http://www.nasa.gov

Visit NASA to access information about its exciting history and present resources.

The Nine Planets
http://seds.lpl.arizona.edu/nineplanets/nineplanets/nineplanets.html

Take a multimedia tour of the solar system and all of its planets and moons.

45

Important Words

capsule a small spacecraft holding one or more astronauts

hatch the door of a spacecraft

manned when there are people on board a spacecraft

mission a goal for spacecraft or astronauts to accomplish

orbit the path a spacecraft travels around the earth

reentry when a spacecraft passes through the earth's atmosphere to land

rocket a powerful vehicle that launches capsules into space

satellite an object that orbits the earth

target rocket a spacecraft in orbit that astronauts find and join up with

unmanned when there are no people on board a spacecraft

Index

(**Boldface** page numbers indicate illustrations.)

Agena rocket, 24, 34, **35, 37, 37, 39**
Aldrin, Edwin E., Jr., 40, **40,** 41
Armstrong, Neil A., **15,** 32, **33**
astronauts, **8**
astronomy, 30
Borman, Frank, 26, 28
capsules, 9, **10, 12,** 13
Cernan, Eugene A., **15,** 34–35
Collins, Michael, 36–37, **37**
computers, 11, **12,** 39
Conrad, Charles, Jr., **14, 22,** 23, 38
Cooper, L. Gordon, Jr., **14,** 22, **22**
food, **26**
fuel cells, 11, 23
Gemini 3, 17–18, **17**
Gemini IV, 19–21
Gemini V, 22–23, **22**
Gemini VI, 24–29, **29**
Gemini VII, 25–29, **29**
Gemini VIII, 31–33, **33**
Gemini IX, 34–35, **35**
Gemini X, 36–38, **37**
Gemini XI, 38–39, **39**
Gemini XII, 40, 41

Gordon, Richard F., Jr., 38, **38**
Grissom, Virgil I., 16
Kennedy, John F., Jr., 6, **7**
launches, **17, 33**
Lovell, James A., Jr., **25,** 26, 28, 40, **40**
McDivitt, James A., **14,** 19, **19**
Moon, **4,** 6, 7, 8, 23, 29, 43
NASA, 6–7, 16, 22, 26, 36, 42
problems, 31–35
Project Apollo, 7–8, 43
Project Gemini, 7–8
Project Mercury, 7–8, 9, 13
Schirra, Walter M., Jr., **14,** 25, **25,** 27, 28
Scott, David R., **15,** 32, **33**
Soviet Union, 5–6
spacecraft, 9–13
space race, 5–6, 43
space suits, **2,** 27
spacewalks, 20–21, **21,** 34–35, 37, 41, **41**
splashdown, **18,** 23, 33, **35**
Stafford, Thomas P., **14, 15,** 25, 27, 28, 34
Titan rocket, 11, **17,** 20
United States, 5–6, 43
White, Edward H., **14,** 19, **19,** 20–21, **21**
Young, John W., 17, 36

Meet the Authors

Paul and Diane Sipiera are a husband and wife who share interests in nature and science. Paul is a professor of geology and astronomy at William Rainey Harper College in Palatine, Illinois. He is a member of the Explorers Club, the New Zealand Antarctic Society, and was a member of the United States Antarctic Research Program. Diane is the director of education for the Planetary Studies Foundation of Algonquin, Illinois. She also manages and operates the STARLAB planetarium program for her local school district.

When they are not studying or teaching science, Diane and Paul can be found enjoying their farm in Galena, Illinois, with their daughters, Andrea, Paula Frances, and Carrie Ann.